A Festival of Birds

sharing with Fleur
loving is what we do.
Best wishes
James

Also by James McGrath from Sunstone Press:

At the Edgelessness of Light, 2005

Speaking With Magpies, 2007

Dreaming Invisible Voices, 2009

Valentines and Forgeries, Mirrors and Dragons, 2011

The Sun is a Wandering Hunter, 2015

A Festival of Birds

Poems
by
James McGrath

SUNSTONE
PRESS

SANTA FE

Cover Art: "Many Birds," Brush and Ink, James McGrath, Tachikawa, Japan, 1978
Cover Photograph: Robert Nugent, Santa Fe, New Mexico
The illustrations in this book are from *Teaching of Brush Strokes* by Morikuni
Tachihana, printed in 1624, reprinted in 1790 and given to James McGrath by his
mentor, Paulette Beall, at the University of Oregon in the late 1940s

I am *Tansu*
I am *Sogetsu*
I am Kabuki
I am Geisha
I am Samurai
I am Lover

Thanks to Frances Hunter, writer friend of Santa Fe, New Mexico, who
edited my manuscript and assisted in the preparation of *A Festival of Birds*.

Sunstone books may be purchased for educational, business, or sales promotional use.
For information please write: Special Markets Department, Sunstone Press,
P.O. Box 2321, Santa Fe, New Mexico 87504-2321.
Printed on acid-free paper

Library of Congress Cataloging-in-Publication Data
Names: McGrath, James, 1928- author.
Title: A festival of birds : poems / by James McGrath.
Description: Santa Fe : Sunstone Press, 2017.
Identifiers: LCCN 2016052457 | ISBN 9781632931719
(softcover : acid-free paper)
Classification: LCC PS3613.C497 A6 2017 | DDC 811/.6--dc23
LC record available at https://lccn.loc.gov/2016052457

SUNSTONE PRESS IS COMMITTED TO MINIMIZING OUR ENVIRONMENTAL IMPACT ON THE PLANET. THE PAPER USED IN THIS BOOK IS FROM
RESPONSIBLY MANAGED FORESTS. OUR PRINTER HAS RECEIVED CHAIN OF CUSTODY (COC) CERTIFICATION FROM: THE FOREST STEWARDSHIP
COUNCIL™ (FSC®), PROGRAMME FOR THE ENDORSEMENT OF FOREST CERTIFICATION™ (PEFC™), AND THE SUSTAINABLE FORESTRY INITIATIVE®
(SFI®). THE FSC® COUNCIL IS A NON-PROFIT ORGANIZATION, PROMOTING THE ENVIRONMENTALLY APPROPRIATE, SOCIALLY BENEFICIAL AND
ECONOMICALLY VIABLE MANAGEMENT OF THE WORLD'S FORESTS. FSC® CERTIFICATION IS RECOGNIZED INTERNATIONALLY AS A
RIGOROUS ENVIRONMENTAL AND SOCIAL STANDARD FOR RESPONSIBLE FOREST MANAGEMENT.

Love is the unnamed bird of Memory.

I dedicate this collection of poems to Betty Yeiko Taira of Okinawa heritage and to Tadao (Rio) Suzuki of Tokyo who gave me these poems through their love, their friendship during the twelve years, and beyond, that I lived in Japan and Okinawa, 1973–1985.

Poet James McGrath with Tadao (Rio) Suzuki, Tokyo, 1985.
Photograph: Katsumaro Fukazawa.

and to my Santa Fe, New Mexico bird-watching friends:

Sheila Gershen
Lonnie Howard
Catherine Ferguson
Mary Soppe
Janet Eigner

Poet James McGrath with Betty Yeiko Taira, Washington DC, 2009.
Photograph: Courtesy of the American Overseas Schools Historical Society Archives, Wichita, Kansas.
Photograph: Lucy Arai Amanson.

Contents

Birds have no fear of darkness
  they are silent composing songs
  for falling stars . . . 57

To write a poem is to love again . . . 91

About the Poet. . . . 93

The Poet Lovers Dream. . . . 95

For an Aspiring Poet . . . 97

Introduction

> There comes a time in the lives of poets
> when they put aside their poems of lost
> love. This gathering is such a give-away.

These poems come from my encounters with the people, the experiences, and the adventures I had within the traditional cultures of the Far East, particularly Japan and Okinawa, and spending time with friends in that unique world.

While working as Arts and Humanities Coordinator with the US Department of Defense Dependents Schools (DODDS) from 1973 through 1985 in Japan, Okinawa, Korea, the Philippines, Taiwan and Midway Island, I found time to study paper-making in the Philippines, temple-painting and kite-making in Korea, and Japanese brush painting, flower arranging, and the flute. I also studied the tea ceremony, earning a Teaching Certificate at the Edo Senkei School.

Most of the poems in *A Festival of Birds* were written during those twelve years. Others were written over the years after my return to my home in New Mexico and just before the publication of this festival collection. For me, memories of beauty and life have no end-time for remembering.

Among my treasured encounters in Japan and Okinawa are those with my beloved friends Tadao (Rio) Suzuki of Tokyo and Betty Yeiko Taira of Okinawa heritage. The gifts these two gave to me came from participating in their daily culture, including attending festivals, visiting temples and shrines, meditating in ancient gardens, gathering seaweed, sharing tea and sushi, and joining in everyday chores. These gifts from Betty and Rio are among the roots and flights of the poems in this collection.

Betty, born in California, was interned with her family and thousands of Japanese Americans under Executive Order 9066 during World War II. She went on from her internment years through American schools to earn a Master's degree from the University of Maryland and to teach classes in the US and to become principal and later an administrator in the Department of Defense Dependents Overseas Schools (DODDS) in the Far East. Betty told me that the years of her internment gave her a wisdom about injustice based on race that she shared with her students and coworkers over the years.

Betty, as a school administrator, and I, as the DODDS Arts Coordinator, created workshops, field trips and classroom adventures for students and teachers based on Asian arts and cultures, particularly Okinawan and Japanese. Together, we participated in tea ceremonies, traditional flower arranging classes and festivals in Okinawa, where we lived as neighbors in Naha, the capital city.

Rio, born in Osaka, Japan, from a long line of Japanese ancestors, met me at a social gathering in Tachikawa, where I lived and worked near the Yokota US Air Base. He was the Cultural Facilitator for the Suntory Company in Tokyo. His interest in American entertainment and culture matched my interest in Japanese culture.

Rio introduced me to Kabuki, Bunraku and Noh Theater. We visited mountain hot springs and craft centers throughout Japan and cooked family meals in his home. He introduced me to his poetry, theater and designer friends. We followed the American Christmas tradition of decorating a tree at a *ryokan* in the Deer Park in Nara with a New Year's Eve all-night celebration at the Meiji Shrine in Tokyo.

When I returned home to New Mexico, Rio would visit me and we would continue to create the poetry of friendship.

When a poem is written in brush and ink on rice paper the words flow as liquidly as clouds forming. This is how many of these poems were written—from the intense, vibrating silence that sings for a poet in a foreign land. I created them in a simple, intense form, not too unlike the traditional haiku or tanka.

Here is the *cheek-cheek-cheek* of the universal sparrow, the *cha-cha-cha* of the bamboo whisk at the edge of a tea bowl. Here a love poem is the scent of winter *mikan* in a New Year's *ofuro*, the touch of falling *sakura* blossoms in Ueno Park, the sliding of autumn shadows across stones in Ryoanji, and the gathering of coral stars on an Okinawa beach.

Earth and sky are filled with the exuberant songs of many birds: a festival of birds. The birds of Japan sing among iris and bamboo. Okinawa island birds sing among hibiscus, coral sands and the drumming of China Sea and Pacific Ocean waves.

Birds fly, sing and nest where and when they will. So poems come to a poet where and when they will. I have been blessed. Poems have come near enough and remained long enough for me to hold, sing, fly and hatch into *A Festival of Birds*.

To share these poems is to love again. I love and endure in a culture that rarely respects the acknowledgement of loving: the intimate sharing between persons. I invite you to remember, to come home to a place you have been before, to sing with the festival of birds in your memory-heart. It takes one feather to know a bird.

—James McGrath, September 2016

Mikan: a sweet-skin-scented orange, the skin used to scent baths
Ofuro: a traditional Japanese bath
Sakura blossoms: cherry blossoms
Ryoanji: the quintessence of Zen art: the sixteenth century garden in Kyoto with
        fifteen stones.
Ryokan: a Japanese inn

My Poems Come at Dawn

When Birds Sing From My Heart

We heard

each other singing

in the clouds

Each poem

I write to you

is my first poem

It is not

the movement of birds

in the bamboo

it is the breath of you

on my neck

Please sing

your dawn song to me

each morning

When the morning

breathes bird songs

I awaken to you

holding me

The moon is covered by a cloud

the light dances

from your eyes

When the sun rises

each morning

you are at the edge

of my dawn

My poems are shaped

by your hand

on my heart

where words are waiting

I cannot

hold my poems unruffled

they are the thrumming waves

of Itoman

Itoman: On the island of Okinawa, Itoman is a coastal town
of fishermen.

After the shadows disappear

in the morning

listen to chattering birds

waiting for you to leave your home

It is a wonder

my writing poems to you

in your silence

To say I love you

    sing like a lark or a dove

    or be silent

In flight

the bird that I am

sings love songs to you

What is more beautiful

the brush of peacock feathers

or our songs

And I smile inside

becoming the songs

that come and go

like falling feathers

in the snow

In the days we were together

I wrote my poems

I was most happy

when I was most sad

I move about

    quietly

    feeling

    the dawn of you

I know you are near

when I find a feather

in the garden

My poems

flow to you

as ink on wet rice paper

I hold my poems

as I hold my breath

in a hibiscus

where birds blush their songs

When I write my poems

to you

the rhythm

is the bamboo whisk

on the edge of a tea bowl

When the Sun is at its Highest

Birds Put their Songs under their Wings

When I look through fox eyes

I see the love-bird

—*sekisei-inko*—

that sings

in your fox eyes

When I listen through fox ears

I hear the love-bird

—*sekisei-inko*—

that sings

in your fox voice

You are the fox

—*kitsune*—

in my garden

Let us bring out of the Spring air

the flower song of finches

I sing at the edge

of your pulsating shadow

as I sing at the edge

of the pulsating gardens of Kyoto

When you

left your *furoshiki* behind

I put it to my lips

Furoshiki: a cloth that may be used to wrap a gift or worn on the shoulders.

Among memories

is the harbinger

of greeting you

at my door

Behind my eyes

    I see your face

    smiling like tea

    in my morning bowl

Behind my ears

    I hear your laughter

    warming my body in sunshine

Behind the tips of my fingers

    I touch your cheeks

    your shoulders

    the tips of your fingers

Behind my thoughts of you

    your poem

    sings on my orange lacquer table

It is enough

    that you read my poems

It is enough

    that you breathe the air I breathe

My loving you

has happened before

iris in *Meiji-jingu*

stone images

pausing late in *Ryoanji*

this loving you

is iris and stone

Meiji-jingu: a major shrine-temple in Tokyo noted for its iris
    garden.

Ryoanji: the quintessence of Zen art; the fifteenth century
    garden in Kyota with fifteen stones.

In the bamboo

part of me

I store all the gifts

you gave to me

In the bamboo part of me

I hear all the songs

you sang to me

In the bamboo part of me

I hold all the silences

you shared with me

There is a cloud

lying in the mountain

caressing the *mikan* of Shizuoka

Mikan: an orange with a strong sweet-scented skin used to
give fragrance to a bath.

Shizuoka: an area of Japan noted for its *mikans*.

My poems say

I love you

my poems are Daisen-in

the Great Sea in Kyoto

Daisen-in: the beautiful white sand garden in Kyoto called
The Great Sea.

There are no words

in my poems

as sweet

as November persimmons

in Nara

There are no words

in my poems

as tranquil

as November deer

in Nara

Nara: the ancient capital of Japan south of Kyoto noted for
the Deer Park and giant Buddha figure

I shall

stop writing poems

when I count

all the grains of coral sand

in Ishigaki

Ishigaki: the island in the Ryukyu Islands near Okinawa
noted for its black pearls and coral sands.

At noon

leaping orange carp

blue dragonflies

in the Meiji Garden

rippling shimmers

flirting cicadas

at night

a quivering moon

silent bird shadows

whispers and splashes

in the Meiji Garden

where we walk

Meiji Garden: an important garden in Tokyo noted for its
irises.

The day

we saw the dead bird

on the road

you said

"that's how death is

all feathery soft"

I believe you

Those side streets

leading to your home

camellias blooming

sparrows bouncing

my feet dancing on stones

In the indelible rhythm

of bird song

my heart sings

Let us write

    the names of the birds

    we hear

    hidden in the clouds

    to remember

    our names

梅に鳩

Birds Have No Fear of Darkness
   They Are Silent Composing Songs
For Falling Stars

Late at night

the moon

arching

is your body

curling toward me

When I greet you

in rare moments

at the end of a day

a gift of a thousand cranes

Your song

is the most pure

among the songs

of many birds

Each night

I walk the earth

in moonlight

your shadow next to me

Without winter *mikan*

in my December bath

the scent of you is lost

Mikan: a sweet scented-skin orange used to give fragrance to
a winter bath.

When you go away

I shall sit in sunshine

watch a rainbow fade

with a breath of rain

There is despair

In my brush

as I write to you

there is sorrow

on my rice paper

as I write to you

I am alone

I shall not search for iris

in Winter

I shall not search for *sakura*

in Spring

I shall not search for *tsutsuji*

in Summer

I shall not search for *shitaki*

in Autumn

I shall not search for you

in clouds

you are here

Sakura: cherry blossoms
Tsutsuji: azalea flowers
Shitaki: a special edible mushroom

I shall take the clay of memory

in my hands

fashion a tear bowl

to hold your passing

Even if I clap my hands

a thousand times

at the Kamakura Shrine

you will not return

Ginkgo leaves turn to gold

before they fall

Kamakura: an ancient city with temples and shrines that have
giant ginkgo trees on the grounds.

You are far away

from the end of my poem

I cannot touch you

It's how love

nested between us

all feathered and tender

shakuhachi breathing

in the garden of four seasons

Shakuhachi: a traditional Japanese bamboo flute.

With my poem

I reach for you

as I reach for a star

My only lament

I never held you

when you went away

Who said

"tomorrow

you have plenty of time"

It was not a bird

If love between us

was disguised

years from now

no one will know

who we were

Now that I am old

when I see your photograph

beside my bed

I remember I was young

We lost time

    we lost one another

    before we started

    did you know it was too late

    to pick persimmons

There are no tears

like falling *sakura* blossoms

in Ueno Park

in April

Sakura blossoms: cherry blossoms.
Ueno Park: a major park in Tokyo where the National Museum and the Panda Bears in the zoo are located.

I wrote your name

in coral sands

the sea holds it secretly

for me

Many birds

    have flown away

    I keep their flight

    in my poems

    to you

There will come a day

tomorrow perhaps

when the pain

of missing you

will cover me

with the feathers of many birds

the pain will be melancholy

filled with the hush of many birds

There will come a day

tomorrow

perhaps

the pain of missing you

will cover me

with the feathers of many birds

I whisper to the wild rose bushes

"please sing again"

I marvel

hearing the songs of meadow larks

how they love the grass in the fields

Birds sing one song

"please remember me"

There is no silence

like the silence

when a bird stops singing

Remember the flock of blackbirds

with iridescent lacquered wings

speaking broken bits of

love poems on your birthday

Your death

and mine

are but falling feathers

I shall return

to you

each night

as the moon returns

to the mountain

Pray

that it is the song of a bird

we hear at the end

Red-winged blackbirds

sing in swamps

calling us back

to where we came from

Tears are gone now

the tear bowl is dry

Winter comes

only the garden receives water

only the cyclamen blooms

To Write a Poem is to Love Again

About the Poet

We are like materialized poems capable
of intense exhilaration and suffering.
—James Hillman, *Form of Character and Lasting Life*, 1999

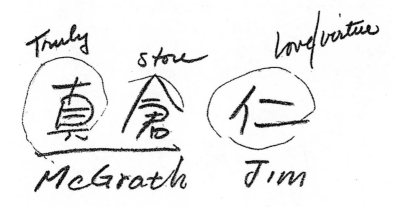

My friend Tadeo translated my name into Japanese symbols, and those symbols had those three meanings: truly, store, love/virtue. What could be better meanings for a poet's name? And my poems do come from the storage (memory) of love, virtue and trust.

A Korean astrologer told me that because I was born on September 2, 1928, I was a Double Dragon. A dragon in the zodiac is the celestial who travels the universe. I have not traveled the universe, but I have been a wanderer in the countries of Greece, Japan, Korea, Yemen, Saudi Arabia, the Congo, China, Bali, Ireland, Chile and Peru and in the mythically-intuitive lands of the Hopi, Navajo and Pueblo people of the Southwest United States.

I have responded to those connections with poetry, paintings, and sculptures and with teaching.

Jonah Raskin said about my connection to the Far East in his biography *James McGrath: In a Class by Himself* that "he [McGrath] could see that, as he put it, Asian life and culture had touched his 'inner soul.' What he once regarded as 'foreign culture' had become over the years an integral part of him . . ."

At the age of eighty-eight, I must continue to acknowledge my storage box of memory. I must continue to respond to the darkness and the light of today's world. I will continue to sing and dance through the darkness and light toward home using the multitude of wings that words in a poem give to me.

The Poet-Lover's Dream

I am Tansu
I am Sogetsu
I am Kabuki
I am Geisha
I am Samurai
I am Mikan
I am Fox
I am Bamboo
I am Iris
I am Noh

I am Persimmon
I am Chrysanthemum
I am Sashimi
I am Cherry Blossoms
I am Plum
I am Chawan
I am Shakuhachi
I am Samisen
I am Fuji
I am Lover

For An Aspiring Poet

James McGrath's response to Dale Harris's question, "Any advice or encouragement for poets coming up?" in her interview in the Summer 2013 *Malpais Review,* is reproduced here:

"No advice but a lot of encouragement to explore and relate to the world you live in. Find the time and space to be quiet, to voice your response. You can write it, dance it, sing it, laugh it, cry it. Your response will be your connection. Respect and share your uniqueness. There is no other voice like yours. Don't be afraid of your darkness and sadness and pains, as well as your laughter and giggles. Each is asking for you to listen, to respond. Get out and experience the world. It is smaller than you think. Fall in love a thousand times. Keep open for spears and kisses. Take backroads and dusty paths. Make up words. Tell lies. Tell truths. Be a friend to animals. Keep flowers on your table. Keep pen and paper nearby. Give your address to strangers. Change your mind and shoes often. Write letters. Acknowledge your teachers because you will become one. Put what you understand is love in everything you do; share it with whomever you meet. Read a lot. Take risks. Keep writing, and it's a good idea to keep your writings somewhere safe. One day they will tell you who you are.'"

James McGrath lives in Santa Fe, New Mexico, USA. In 2008, he was designated a Santa Fe Living Treasure. In 2010, he was awarded the Institute of Indian Arts Visionary Award. In 2012, he was given the Gratitude Award by the New Mexico Literary Arts for his contribution to the literary life of New Mexico. In 2015, the University of Baltimore's Passager editors awarded him its 2015 Poet Award.

This book of poetry has been set
in Poliphilus MT Pro.

A revival based on the Hypnerotomachia Poliphili,
"published by Aldus Manutius in Venice in 1499, using a type
that had been cut by Francesco Griffo"
Poliphilus is an exact copy of fifteenth century printing
on hand made paper." [Linotype]

Made under the direction of Stanley Morison
at Monotype as Series 170 in 1923.

CPSIA information can be obtained
at www.ICGtesting.com
Printed in the USA
FSOW01n0357280317
32302FS